Mugworts in May

a folklore of herbs

by LINDA OURS RAGO

D1559920

quarrier
press

Charleston, West Virginia

Library of Congress
Catalog Card No. 95-69494

ISBN 13 : 978-0-9646197-0-8
ISBN 10 : 0-9646197-0-9

10 9 8 7 6 5 4 3 2 1

TYPOGRAPHY Arrow Graphics
COVER PAINTING Betty Warner
COVER DESIGN Bill Vaughn
DIGITAL REFORMATTING Mark S. Phillips

Distributed by :

1125 Central Avenue
Charleston, WV 25302
www.wvbookco.com

Mugworts in May

a folklore of herbs

by Linda Ours Rago

"O, mickle is the powerful grace that lies
In plants, herbs, stones and their true qualities."

—SHAKESPEARE, *Romeo and Juliet*, II 3

*With honor to Muriel and Lula Catherine and
all the Grandmothers*

Table of Contents

Introduction

GREEN TENDRIL weaves through the fabric of time. When animal life first pushed up from the mud of chaos, simple plants were already there to welcome us into the web of life. The mystical forces of their creation are tied forever with our own. Our forbears have handed down knowledge of the unseen and inexplicable influences of plants on humankind. This knowledge comes to us in lore, empirical knowledge, and intuition. In this day and time, people often associate a plant-centered spirituality only with Native Americans and other indigenous peoples. However, the spirit world has been strongly tied to botanical life throughout Western civilization.

Herbs were of great importance in the religious ceremonies and curing rituals of our European ancestors long before, and well into, medieval times. Green herbs guided them through birth, life, and death. The ideas underlying white or good magic were: to be in harmony with the natural world; to stay healthy and happy; to protect ourselves from malevolent elements; and to prepare ourselves for death and the journey of our souls to peace.

The roots of herbal magic are ancient, but they have almost been lost through the years. Except for the work of a handful of scholars, very little ancient herbal knowledge exists in written form. Early oral chroniclers, like the Grimm brothers, held that the roots of herbal mysticism in Europe were in pre-Christian mythology. Two of the writings of poet and scholar Robert Graves, *The White Goddess* and *The Greek Myths*, shed light on ancient herbal history. Graves' works tied the Celtic and Mediterranean herbal traditions together. Recently, UCLA archaeologist Marija Gimbutus, in *The Language of the Goddess,* found that her mythical and poetic studies of herbs almost magically align with those of Graves, the Grimms, and others.

This book, however, will part from the scholars and explore the herbal knowledge passed from parent to child, grandparent to grandchild, and friend to friend. It will try to pick up some of the old threads: some frayed, some violently torn, and others surprisingly strong and green.

In the northern forests of Europe, the beliefs surrounding herbs existed side by side with early Christianity for many centuries. Monks tending monastery gardens and "Wise Women" in the villages and countryside faithfully employed herbal knowledge. The monks even attempted to "Christianize" much of the knowledge of plant cultivation and use—along with its lore, charms and spells. *In nomen*

Patris, Filii et Spiritus Sancti—In the name of the Father, Son, and Holy Spirit—was commonly recited by the monks as herbs were plucked for cures.

The early church in Europe, however, eventually made a zealous effort to obliterate these ancient doctrines that honored the spirit of the earth. Later, the changes wrought by the 18th century mechanistic view of the world, closely followed by the Industrial Revolution, caused these herbal traditions to be all but lost.

[3]

The strength and persistence of a particular aspect of this nearly forgotten culture—herb lore—fascinates me. This fascination has held throughout my nearly thirty years as a traditional Appalachian herb woman. During that time, I have found both folklore and oral history to be rich in direct and encoded knowledge of the plant world's mystical relationship with us.

Many early writings, particularly from England in the 15th through the 17th centuries, hint at the enduring strength of people's belief in the sovereignty of the earth. Unfortunately, our forebears were eventually taught to fear the traditional Wise Woman and her repository of oral knowledge. Fear of her supposed supernatural powers, herbal secrets, and medicinal remedies—and their powerful capabilities—was instilled by men who felt threatened by the Wise Woman.

But her powers linger, quietly and persistently filling small corners of our everyday life. Who hasn't looked for four-leaved clovers? Do we sprinkle sage in our Thanksgiving turkey dressing simply because it tastes good? How many of us have a pot of hens and chicks by the back door? These seemingly insignificant activities are part of our ancient heritage. Found by those of us blessed with the "second sight," four-leaved clovers draw us closer to the sprites of the meadow. Grandmothers whisper, nearly inaudibly, that garden sage imparts wisdom and soothes an overtaxed digestive tract. Those hens and chicks keep

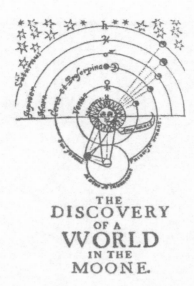

THE
DISCOVERY
OF A
VVORLD
IN THE
MOONE.

away lightning and produce a soothing balm for burns, say the Wise Women.

Much of our herb lore comes from a distant time (the Iron Age and before) when the moon played a more important role in ordering our lives. Time was kept according to the lunar agricultural calendar. This calendar was based on nature's cycles of thirteen 28-day months and one extra day. Hence, we hear the expression, "a year and a day."

Magical and medicinal herbs were often gathered at night. Some were gathered when the moon was waxing, others when it was waning or in eclipse. For example, moonwort was gathered only during the full moon to ensure its full potency. The influence of the moon on many of our biological functions is now widely accepted. Our ancestors knew what they were doing. "We humans are food for the moon," wrote a Chinese sage. This holds true for plants as well.

To my mind, herbs are the most intimate of our green friends. Usually these little gray or green plants do not fuel our bodies like grains and vegetables. However, they have been closely linked with the energy of our healing, our spirits, and our emotions for eons. Indeed, many of the Greek herbal practices employed in the temples of Aesculapius (the Greek god of medicine) are still recognizable in our herbal folk traditions. Herbs remain firmly entwined on every coil of the spiral of our lives: from conception, through celebration, to death.

At the present time, humankind's very existence depends upon our respect for the sovereignty of the earth. Our ancestors served as guardians of practical information and mystical herb lore. We should give them our gratitude for the secrets they have held (often at great personal risk) and passed to us. Those ancestors were quite often the oldest and wisest among us—the Wise Women. It is for us now to cherish and tend our plants and pass the mysteries on to another generation of garden keepers—wise women and wise men.

The Wise Woman's Garden

Madam, wol ye stalk
Pryvely into the garden to see the herbs grow?
And forth they wend
Passing forth softly into the herbery.
—CHAUCER

SUNFLOWERS AND ROSES, rosemary and thyme, all run riot in the Wise Woman's garden. Tubs of fat sedum and towering hollyhocks crowd the stone path. In times only shortly gone by, every village or town had a recognized Wise Woman. Her house was usually the last one before orderly streets gave way to meadows and hedgerow. Her garden was a place to stop for sprigs of catnip to soothe the colicky baby; a leaf of mugwort to slip in the shoe to ease sore feet; and maybe even some lunaria florets to ensure prosperity.

CHAPTER ONE

The Wise Woman and her garden were the repository of untold centuries of folk wisdom and knowledge gained by trial and error. More often than not she was a midwife, healer, and layer-out of the dead as well. New Englanders called the Wise Woman *goodwife*. In Virginia she was called *granny*. In the lowland South she was usually an African-American woman, enriching the European traditions with African wisdom and recipes.

Wise Women from all over would frequently prescribe one herb for a multitude of different symptoms or charms. The herbs that she dispensed for protection from bad luck or evil vapors, she also used for healing practices. For example, chamomile chases away nightmares, but also eases an upset stomach. The Wise Woman's ability to accurately utilize one herb for an infinite number of uses should come as no surprise. An ancient relationship has always existed between women and plants.

This relationship weaves through our notions of flowers, gardening, botany, "green witchcraft," and Mother Earth herself. The idea of the female engendering fertility—and the Earth Mother nurturing plants—is deeply embedded in our collective psyche. Scholars, such as Joseph Campbell and Robert Graves, contend that this thinking is a vestige of the "mystery religions." The mystery religions were based on a great veneration for all living things, and flourished in Mediterranean culture between the third and second millennia B.C. An even older reference to this relationship are the Cro-Magnon cave paintings. These paintings repeatedly depict, with exuberance and beauty, the motif of the female figure as Mother Earth.

In the current post-industrial age we can still find a Wise Woman or two in quiet country lanes, as well as in our imaginations, memories, and family histories. Until only a few years ago, Florence Williamson in Woodville, Virginia, tended a marvelous garden. She was known for sharing wisdom along with her plants. One afternoon when I dropped in, she was gathering raspberry leaves to brew in a tea for a friend having "women's troubles." Many people remember her driving up to speak at Garden Club meetings in her battered old station wagon, which would always be stuffed with flowers and herbs.

Just over the ridge, in West Virginia, a round motherly lady keeps a Wise Woman's garden. She always gives advice along with her plant cuttings. The latter she hands you in a rusted soup can. "Now when you cut your children's hair, be sure to scratch the clippings in around your lavender roots." She plants by the moon, setting great store in astrology. Since she considers my husband's and my astrological signs entirely incompatible, she always tilts her head to one side and asks, "Are you and your man still getting on?"

I myself am often called on to speak about herbs

at Garden Clubs and other meetings. While there, I nearly always learn as much as I share. Women today still have a strong oral history. The elderly Judy sisters in Pendleton County, West Virginia, said that they would never plant parsley themselves because it is bad luck, foretelling of death. However, if they piled parsley seed on the fence post and let the wind sow the seed, bad luck vanished.

"If you steal a plant it will thrive best and bring good luck," is an adage I have heard from my mother and many others. I have a theory to explain it. For hundreds of years, women were burned at the stake for simply having knowledge of plant mysteries. Giving or receiving a plant "with powers" could be damning evidence against either party. It was safer to steal such plants than to purposefully give them to another. Rue is an herb with an ancient history of mystical powers. More than once a modern matron has told me, "Now I'll turn my head while you take a cutting of that rue plant." Some Roman Catholics still use rue today in the sprinkling of holy water.

Recently a friend told me how her mother would always send out for a few mullein leaves just before company came. The prickly leaves rubbed on her cheeks gave them a pink glow before cosmetics were available or socially acceptable. Yellow stalks of mullein grow as weeds on the roadside. They were originally brought from Europe, and carefully tended as medicinal plants. The leaves were dried and smoked to cure respiratory ailments.

An elderly Appalachian woman once reminded me never to bring in just one of any flower, it being the worst of luck. Along these lines is the adage that plants should never be gathered in even numbers:

always gather three or five of each stalk. This old saying has historical underpinnings. The number three is of critical symbolic importance in both the Christian Trinity and in the Triple Goddess aspect of the ancient lunar-based religions. The number five has special significance in the Celtic traditions.

Now we shall depart from general herbal history and focus on the folklore of specific herbs in the Wise Woman's garden. The garden in this book is imaginary, made up of the corners and patches of many gardens. However, all of the plants and trees mentioned are as real as the wise women who have passed this knowledge down through the centuries. The sources are as modern as books, old and new. They are also as ancient as intuition and wisdom from the heart, passed down in the spoken word. Let's enter the garden.

Standing at the southern end of the Wise Woman's garden is a birch tree, one of the many varieties growing in North America. In myth and legend the birch tree grows at the entrance to Paradise. It is also known as the tree of inception. Birch rods are used to drive away the Spirit of the Old Year—a metaphor seen in the use of birch twig brooms.

Just inside the protective garden gate grows tall angelica *(Angelica archangelica)*. It is believed to have a heavenly origin; its powers are greatly revered. Poets make crowns of it for inspiration. Roots of angelica hung around our necks protect against enchantments. Angelica prefers rich soil and sunshine, but will tolerate more shade than most herbs.

Nodding blue borage flowers *(Borago officinalis)* brighten the path into the garden proper. This herb imparts courage to those who carry it, or drink tea or ale in which it has been steeped. "I Borage, give Courage" is the ancient phrase of renown. It also encourages cheerfulness. Borage likes rich soil and sunshine, and will reseed itself several times a season for a continuous display of achingly vivid blue.

Pungent basil *(Ocimum basilicum)* grows in the sunniest spot of the garden. Avoid eating too much basil, for it will dull the eyesight. Young men and women, when blinded by love, should present a bouquet of basil to their lover as a symbol of passion. Another adage is that the touch of a fair lady will restore wilted basil. Remember that basil

seed will not germinate unless sown with verbal abuse!

Carnations, or clove gillyflowers *(Dianthus caryophyllus)* grow in the driest and rockiest part of the garden. This old-fashioned plant represents gentleness. Historically it was used as a symbolic rent. St. Andrew's Monastery in Northampton, England, paid rent in three gillyflowers at the time of the Protectorate under Oliver Cromwell. The carnation will fade if the mistress of the garden dies. The delicate gillyflower is actually a sturdy rock garden plant that prefers full sun and good drainage.

Between the paving stones of the Wise Woman's garden grows chamomile *(Anthemis nobilis).* The herb's blooms are bright yellow, as they were in ancient Egypt, where it was dedicated to the sun. Peter Rabbit's mother is one of many who uses chamomile tea to settle an upset stomach, ease sleeplessness, and chase away nightmares. It is a favorite in garlands because it symbolizes the ability to bounce back after adversity. Chamomile likes sunshine, but will tolerate a little shade.

By the kitchen door grows a row of chives *(Allium schoenoprasum)*. Chives have a lineage of over 5000 years. Ancient Egyptians held chives sacred; the herb is pictured on their monuments. King Oberon's elfin troop puff on tiny pipes made of hollow chive stems. Gypsies tell fortunes with the dried stalks by casting them into patterns. Chives will grow almost anywhere! They seem to enjoy being crowded in with other herbs.

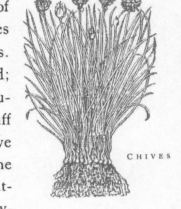

CHIVES

Coriander *(Coriandrum sativum)* or cilantro, is best known for its culinary uses. However, the herb also has a magical history. Biblical references cite the seed as "like manna," the divine food. Evil sorcerers once used coriander to conjure up mischief. Coriander requires full sun.

The huge yellow discs in the Wise Woman's garden are not sunflowers, but elecampane *(Inula helenium)*. The dried roots of the herb are used as a cough remedy. Fairies particularly like elecampane, hence its nickname, elfdock. In many images of Helen of Troy, you will see the mythical beauty carrying a stalk of the herb as Paris whisks her away. Grow elecampane by a fence or wall, where it has something to lean on.

Every Wise Woman grows garlic *(Allium liliaceae)* because it is the most potent folk symbol against evil. Legend says that when Satan stepped out of the Garden of Eden after the fall of man and woman, garlic sprang up from the spot where he placed his left foot. Garlic was sacred to the ancients. Homer credits garlic with saving Ulysses from being turned into a pig by Circe. Plant garlic bulbs in the autumn just like tulips or daffodils.

Flax *(Linum)* appears as a bright spot of blue in the garden. It is the herb of Hulda, the Teutonic goddess who first taught mortals to spin and weave. Hulda visits and blesses the earth twice a year: once in summer, when the flax blooms; and once in winter, during the mysterious twelve nights just before the Feast of Epiphany. Children who dance in the flax flowers will grow up to be beautiful and possessed of supernatural skills. Flax is lovely in a perennial border.

Every country garden has feverfew *(Chrysanthemum parthenium)* growing against the fence, where a clump will entice the fairies. Also known as bridesbutton, it is a traditional addition to the bridal bouquet. Feverfew cleanses the house and wards off disease. Applied to the head, it purges a siege of melancholy. Feverfew is often recommended to alleviate the troublesome symptoms of menopause. It does

FEVERFEW

well in the sun, and likes to grow in old pots.

On the east side of the Wise Woman's garden grows elder *(Alnus glutinosa)*, a magical herb tree. An elder tree mother lives in each tree and watches over it. Ask permission before cutting this tree, or bad luck will follow. If you stand near an elder on Midsummer's Eve, prepare to see Toly, the King of Elves, and his procession. Elder branches burned on Christmas Eve will reveal all sorcerers in the neighborhood. A cross of elder twigs hung in the barn protects the animals inside. Carrying a sprig in your pocket is a charm against rheumatism. Gypsies say that cutting elder branches for firewood is bad luck, but that anything made of elder is good luck. To safeguard against evil, stand inside a magic circle on Twelfth Night (January 6) with elder catkins (the flowers of the elder tree) you gathered on the spring equinox.

Enclosing the Wise Woman's garden is a fragrant white hawthorn *(Crataegus oxyacantha)* hedge. It protects from bad luck and mischievous spirits. Destroying an ancient hawthorn is believed to cause loss of money, cattle and children! Hawthorn blossoms are traditionally used in the wedding bouquet. The blossoms also summon the hawthorn spirit, Maia, the goddess of wisdom and the winds. Some scholars say our word "hedge" actually comes from the word "hag" or old woman, referring to the spirit or mother of the hedge. Incidentally, always cut a hedge from east to west, the path of the sun.

SEDUM

The tub of sedum by the back door is one of the Wise Woman's plants that gives the most protection from misfortune. It has a myriad of folk names: hens and chicks, old man and old woman, houseleeks, and stone crop. By any name it will protect a home from lightning when it grows in the garden or on a wall.

Lady's mantle *(Alchemilla vulgaris)* is the graceful plant cascading over the Wise Woman's pool. If a girl-child's face is washed each morning with the dew that collects in the center of a lady's mantle leaf, she will grow to be beautiful. Dawn is the hour at which the dew has its most magical properties.

The bending willow *(Salix)* tree loves water; it grows in the moist part of the Wise Woman's garden. It is the home of the willow mother, who is the inspiration for all the arts. The old adages are, "Burn not willow, a tree sacred to Poets," and "Gifts of eloquence can be received by touching the willow trees."

The low-growing hedge of lavender *(Lavandula officinalis)* is the symbol of truth and purity. Lavender flowers quilted in a cap comfort the brain. A few twigs tossed into a Midsummer's Eve bonfire will protect the family all year.

Two large hemlocks *(Conim maculatum)* grow beside the northern door of the Wise Woman's cottage. Almost everyone knows hemlock is poisonous and should never be ingested. But the Wise Woman knows that hemlock grown outside the home will keep the family healthy and sound by absorbing any evil which might be about.

The beautiful, white, arching branches in the far corner of the garden are meadowsweet *(Spiraea ulmaria)*, also known as queen of the meadow or brideswort. In the 16th century it was said of meadowsweet

> The leaves and flowers excell all other herbs for to deck up houses, strew in chambers, hall and banqueting houses in summertime; for the smell thereof makes the heart merrie and delightethe the senses.
> —JOHN GERARD, *The Herbal*, 1597.

When meadowsweet is thrown into a pond on Midsummer's Eve it will help to reveal a thief: sinking, it points to a man; floating, the thief is a woman.

Lowly mugwort *(Artemisia vulgaris)* is extremely magical: placing a sprig in your shoe will prevent weariness. However, a sprig in your shoe on Midsummer's Eve will cause you to be carried upon the back of a white horse. At daylight, the horse will disappear and leave you stranded! Growing under the mugwort is a coal, which offers protection from plague, lightning, and carbuncles. A wreath of mugwort protects from

evil. Eating mugwort in May brings good health all summer. Natives of Scotland say that eating mugwort will protect you from paying too many bills.

Pennyroyal *(Mentha pulegium)* is always put into the crèche at Christmas because it will burst into bloom at midnight. It is a great protection from the evil eye. Husbands and wives who have fallen out should offer one another pennyroyal as atonement. In the 16th century Gerard wrote "A garland of pennie royal made and worne on the head is good against headaches and giddiness." John Gerard, *The Herbal*.

The sprawling ground cover on the shady slope of the Wise Woman's garden is periwinkle *(Vinca)*. The French call this magical plant *violette de sorcier*. The Germans call it the flower of immortality. The Wise

Woman knows that if a man and a woman eat these leaves together, love will grow between them.

In the spring garden grow primroses *(Primula),* the restorers of lost beauty; and pansies *(Viola),* which provoke thought and cheerfulness.

The queen of the Wise Woman's garden is the rose. The rose is associated with the goddesses Venus and Aphrodite. It is the flower of women and the plant of love potions. Following is some "rose lore" with advice for young girls seeking to know about their future love.

ROSE

Upon midnight at Midsummer's Eve, go into the garden backward without speaking a word. Gather a rose, place it in a clean sheet of paper, not looking at it until Christmas. At Christmas wear it stuck in your bosom, and the man who plucks it out will be your future true love.

By the Wise Woman's southernmost doors of her house and barn we find rowan *(Sorbus).* Rowan is the tree of life and a tree of great power. Folk names are quickbeam, wichen, witchwood and witchbane. This small mountain tree, tied with a red thread, offers great protection for the family. It is particularly effective in shielding animals from spells. Some folks believe that bewitched horses can only be controlled with a crop made of rowan branches.

Against a sunny, protected wall grows sesame *(Sesamum orientale)*, or benne. This tasty herb from Africa brings good luck. Also growing here is yarrow *(Alchillea millefolium)*, which staunches bleeding. Its feathery leaves will tremble when a wicked sorcerer comes near.

"How can one die who grows sage in the garden?" is an old adage, *"Cur morietur homo cui Salvia Crescit in Horto?"* Sage *(Salvia)* promotes a happy home. Where sage thrives, the woman rules. Sir Frances Bacon said toads love to sit under sage bushes.

The sunlit places of honor in the Wise Woman's garden are given to rosemary *(Rosmarinus)* and thyme *(Thymus)*. Rosemary is the symbol of friendship, love and remembrance. Although it is dedicated to the Virgin Mary, it was cherished long before the advent of Christianity. The ancients tied rosemary twigs on a baby's cradle to ensure sweet dreams. Grandfathers still drink rosemary tea to grow hair on shiny heads.

Thyme is the ancient plant of energy and magic. Almost every charm to see fairies and wood elves includes thyme. Fairies lay their sleeping babies on thyme blossoms when they go dancing at night. To encourage the wee folk back into your garden in the Spring, set out little bowls of thyme on May Eve. Just being near thyme is said to renew the spirits—its

fragrance has been called "dawn in paradise."

Along the path leading out of the Wise Woman's garden is wormwood *(Artemisia absinthium)*. Like all silvery artemisias (a genus of herbs), it was named for the moon goddess Diana, who found the plant and delivered its powers to Chiron the Centaur. The Wise Woman knows that wormwood counteracts the effects of poisoning from toadstools, hemlock, shrews, and dragons. It also draws down the power of the moon.

Curled up sunning herself on the Wise Woman's gatepost is Blackberry. Blackberry is a tortoiseshell cat born on Michaelmas (September 19), the luckiest birthday for cats. Sometimes these tri-colored kittens born on Michaelmas are called money cats—they guarantee that your pockets are always full of coins.

At the very end of the Wise Woman's lane is the ancient oak tree *(Quercus)*, an important and revered tree. Virgil tells of the belief that the roots of the oak go down as deep into the earth as its branches reach upward to the sky. This is symbolic of a deity whose powers extend to the underworld and the heavens.

OAK

The Enchanted Hedgerow

Herbs from the Dark Side of the Moon,
or *Poisonous Herbs*

THE LIST OF PLANTS found in the Wise Woman's garden is long. However, it is not complete without the list of the dangerous herbs and roots she gathers from the hedgerow. The tales of harm they have wrought from their dark and secret places has, over the ages, overshadowed the knowledge of their good and kindly uses. **When administered with care, knowledge, and caution** these herbs have powerful properties of healing and protection. "Whatever you give forth comes back to you threefold," is the Wise Woman's maxim, along with "That which kills, also cures." Most of the dangerous herbs can be useful when they are properly applied in minute doses, by good and learned folk seeking only to relieve suffering. Let's examine some

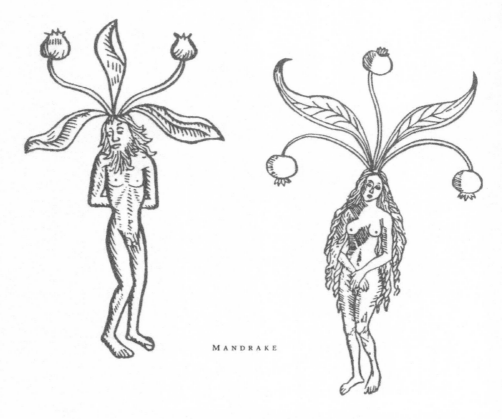

MANDRAKE

of the dangerous and legendary herbs from the dark side.

Mandrake *(Mandragora officinarum)*

The mandrake and the tales surrounding it are as mysterious and enticing as any from the enchanted hedgerow. However, it is actually a relatively harmless medicinal plant. Mandrake is one of our earliest known herbs. It has been found in royal chambers in the Egyptian pyramids as a talisman. Mandrake was described in the ancient text, *Ebers Papyrus*, in approximately 1700–1600 B.C.

The Bible mentions mandrake twice. In Genesis XXX 14–16, Rachel bartered with Leah for the mandrake roots so that she might become fruitful. In the Song of Solomon VII 11–13, the lovely young Shulammite invited her beloved to go out into the country to retrieve the perfumed mandrake, which would make them ardent in their love. Mandrake is an ancient aphrodisiac, particularly valued if the root takes the shape of a man or woman.

Throughout the Middle Ages, mandrake was highly regarded as a painkiller. Today we have evidence as to why it may relieve pain. The plant contains an alkaloid that may cause hallucinations, presumably relieving some symptoms of pain through its "mood-altering" ability. Over the centuries, dozens of bizarre legends have been told about the harvesting of the mandrake root. For example, to dig up the root, draw a circle around the plant with a sword. The digging, however, can only be accomplished with a favorable wind blowing. Another myth is that a dog must be tied to the root to pull it out. This is so the unveiled evil will befall the poor dog instead of the human. The strangest and most widely held belief is that the mandrake root shrieks like a human when torn from the earth. Lawyers take note: a mandrake root tucked in the right armpit of a party to a lawsuit guarantees a successful verdict.

Shakespeare knew well the tales and mystery surrounding the mandrake. Juliet feared that when she awakened in the tomb she would shriek "like mandrakes torn out of the earth." *Romeo and Juliet*, iv. 3, 47. Cleopatra cried "Give me to drink Mandrake . . . That I might sleep out this great cap of time . . . My Antony is away." *Antony and Cleopatra*, i. 5, 4.

To cultivate mandrake, sow the seeds in light soil shortly after the berries ripen. Transplant the seedlings carefully to a sunny, well-drained spot. Mulch it with sprigs of green spruce from autumn until early spring.

Hemlock
Water Hemlock *(Cicutaria palustris)*
Evergreen Hemlock *(Conium maculatum)*

POISON HEMLOCK

Many of us have read that it was hemlock juice with which Socrates killed himself in 399 B.C. Scholars think it was actually a mixture of water hemlock, wine and laudanum. In Greek culture at that time, poisoning by deadly herbs was the common way by which criminals were put to death. The ancient

Greek physician Dioscorides, however, wrote that proper minuscule doses of hemlock relieved pain in mother's breasts, and weakened sexual appetites. Herbalist John Gerard wrote in 1597 that leaves applied externally would prevent young girls' breasts from growing, and prevent young boys from reaching sexual maturity. Hemlock was often grown in monastery gardens to subdue the lust of the flesh of the lonely monks. Long before the time of monks, however, it was the custom to plant hemlock trees outside the home. From its station outside the door, the hemlock absorbs any poison that might be about, keeping the family healthy. How many of us still have the protective hemlock growing by the door? Note: **Both versions of hemlock, if ingested, are highly toxic!**

Monkshood *(Aconitum napellus)*

Also known as wolfbane, this is the most dangerous of the poisonous herbs. It only takes a few monkshood flowers to kill a human. All parts of the plant are poisonous! Monkshood is a lovely garden plant, grown in many borders. However, know its deadly power. Be sure children have no access to monkshood.

An early folk name for monkshood is elfbolt. Early Celtic hunters used the quick-acting poison on arrow tips. During the first World War, aconitine, a derivative of monkshood, was used as a substitute for the painkiller morphine. Minute doses of monkshood are still used as a heart stimulant in homeopathic medicines. Be wary of monkshood, however, because even today **there is no antidote for its deadly poison.**

Thornapple *(Datura stramonium)*

Often called "Sorcerer's Herb," this poisonous plant was one of the earliest plants to accompany the European settlers to America. Its presence was recorded as early as 1679 in Jamestown. Historical records say it was accidentally added to the soldiers soup. The soldiers grew violent, lost consciousness, and became gravely ill. Because of this Jamestown connection, thornapple is also called Jimson Weed. Thornapple was commonly used in love-philtres, or love potions; but the line between arousal and death was a fine one.

Nightshade *(Atropa belladonna)*

This poisonous herb is named for the Greek Fate *Atropos,* the inflexible one who cuts the thread of life. Deadly nightshade was often the scissors of her hand. Nightshade is also known as belladonna—the old

GARDEN NIGHTSHADE

Italian name—meaning "servant of love and beauty." This meaning comes from its use by vain southern European ladies in search of large, dreamy eyes. The atropine in the herb dilates the pupils. Therefore, the women diluted belladonna juice in water, and used it as eye drops. Today physicians sometimes prescribe belladonna in tiny amounts as a sedative. A magical tale of belladonna is that the plant can change into a beautiful woman who is deadly to meet on a deserted road. Note: **all parts of the plant are extremely poisonous.** It is best if we all avoid her on the roadside!

Henbane *(Hyoseyamus niger)*

Among other herbs which are poisonous and
harmful, henbane is not the least, so that the
common man, not without fear, should spit at the
herb when he hears its name spoken, not to
mention when he sees it growing in great quantity
where his children play.

—SIMON PAULLI, *Flora Danica*, 1648

The Spaniards brought the potato and tomato
back from the New World in the 16th century. The
Spaniards believed the plants to be poisonous: they
looked just like their own deadly henbane. The ugly
hairy-stemmed henbane is sometimes called devil's
pouch or dog-piss root. Its history is as old as
civilization itself. Henbane is first mentioned in the
Ebers Papyrus of ancient Egypt, where it is described
as dangerous. The name henbane refers to the use
which gypsies found for the herb. They could snatch
away drowsy chickens from a hen house filled with the
hypnotic, soporific fumes of smoldering henbane.

Flying Ointments

This name refers to those herbs and mix-
tures rumored to help "witches" fly through

 the night. At the beginning of the 15th century, the Christian church earnestly began its battle—and propaganda—against the Wise Women. Therefore, many people believed that the Wise Women were witches, and could actually fly through the night on broomsticks. Sometimes they were said to turn into owls and fly as well. Today, stories of these broomstick rides have taken on mythic proportions. It should be remembered, however, that spiritualists from almost every culture and religion have claimed that the soul can make journeys while the physical body stays at home.

We live in an exciting time when one scientific law after another totters and falls to new discoveries. However, our knowledge of the soul in relation to the brain is too inadequate to explain such mysteries as premonition, intuition, creativity, love, or spiritual journeys.

The fact remains that at certain times of the astrological year, early herbalists brewed "flying ointments" from special plants. These ointments let them fly to their great gatherings in the mountains. We now think the narcotic effect of the herbs created the sensation of flying, and that these early herbalists were "tripping" narcotically. In the Middle Ages, women were sometimes found—unconscious and sick—by their families, while they later insisted they had been flying about.

Herbal flying ointment recipes have been handed down to us from many sources, but none of them are complete. However, **all of them contain highly toxic herbs that can be deadly!** Some of the most commonly cited herbs in these ointments include: water hemlock, celery, parsley, watercress, iris, water lily, cinquefoil, potentilla, monkshood, poppy, deadly nightshade, mandrake, thornapple, spurge, lettuce, purslane and poplar.

Shakespeare's Brew

William Shakespeare knew well the herbs of his time and place. Nearly all of his works are rich in herbal lore. In his tragedy *Macbeth*, we find the most famous deadly herbal mixture of all time.

> Eye of newt, and toe of frog,
> Wool of bat, and tongue of dog,
> Adder's fork, and blind-worm's sting,
> Lizard's leg and howlet's wing . . . .
> —*Macbeth*, iv., 1

The words of the bard conjure images of animal parts, but in all likelihood most of them were herbs. Certainly "adder's fork" is adder's tongue *(Ohioglossum vulgatum)*, a small fern that was highly regarded as medicinal and magical. It carried the aura of mysticism because it was felt to bear the seed of invisibility. "Tongue of dog" is hound's tongue *(Cynoglossom officinale)*. To enter unnoticed into a house guarded by dogs, one had only to sprinkle hound's tongue leaves about the door.

Not only did our ancestors understand these encoded references to animals, but they knew the power of "Root of hemlock digged in the dark" and "Slips of yew, silvered in the moon's eclipse." *Macbeth*, iv, 1.

In our age, however, listen to the bard's lines in *Henry IV*, ii:

> The united vessel of their blood
> Mingled with reason of suggestion
> (As force perforce, the age will pour it in)
> Shall never leak, though it do work as strong
> As aconitum or rash gunpowder.

Today few of us believe that an herb is as powerful as a gun. Neither may we know that slips of yew are magical. But few will deny the dark powers of herbs such as heroin or tobacco—which still cast their deadly spells from the dark side.

CHAPTER THREE

Herbal Charms—A History

SHORT RHYMES invoking the aid of plants are traditionally called "charms." I have been gathering these "charming" little ditties for many years. My collection grows larger by the season. Endless varieties appear on common themes. The charms are passed by word of mouth, with many folks adding their own twists. It is amazing to me how many are still being shared from person to person.

Today's herbal charms come to us with hints of their historical roles. A traditional charm arises from the day set aside in April as "Hoke Day," in English-speaking countries, and *"Hockzeit"* or "Wedding Day" in German. On this day, women were put in charge, and recited "ancient herbal charms." Is this an Anglo-Saxon vestige of an earlier matriarchal culture? Scholars contend that most of the existing English charms are Anglo-Saxon in origin. However, others abound, including ancient Celtic ritual chants such as "High Ho" or "Hey Diddle Diddle"—which many scholars translate as "Sing words clear, sing unclear."

Women have been notoriously undereducated, at least formally, for centuries. It is for this reason that the Wise Woman herbal charm tradition is primarily oral. It is also the reason the Wise Women pass the knowledge in rhyme: it makes for easier recollection. This is not the language of scholarly books or pedantic speech. It is, however, a language of vivid images which evoke emotions. This is the best kind of poetry. The charms do not follow the rules of punctuation, grammar or tense; they are a non-linear language.

Poetic rhyming and imagery are the language that bridge the left-brain consciousness of reason with the right-brain consciousness of dreams and emotions. This is why poetry is so powerful. Rhythm, rhyme, and repetition in language are relaxing and hypnotic. Poetry opens doors deep within our consciousness. Here wishes are brought into reality. Our ancestors intuitively understood that great things may be wrought by the simplest.

I have placed the charms in this book into several categories. You will notice that many crossovers occur, and that some charms could be in every category—magic is elusive! An adage about charms is that if you repeat them seven times they become a spell. Of course, if you tell anyone about your spell, it will not come true!

CHAPTER FOUR

Herbal Charms for Aid and Protection

HERBAL CHARMS for aid and protection were invoked to bring us prosperity, happiness, and protection from things that go bump in the night.

St. John's Wort, scaring from the midnight heath
The witch and goblin with its spicy breath.
> —Traditional

I, Borage,
Give courage.
> —Traditional charm to be recited while picking
> the blue borage blossoms.

Mower, mower, finest of all
With this fennel, you'll purr, not stall.
> —English charm guaranteed to be "sovereign"
> to start a power mower, to be recited with fennel
> in left hand, saluting mower.

Eldest of worts,
Thou hast might for three
And against thirty
For venom availest
For flying vile things
That through the land rove.

> —Traditional charm invoking the mugwort's protection, also found in the Saxon manuscript in the Harleian collection in The British Museum.

Trefoil, Johnswort, Vervaine, Dill
Hinder witches of their will.

> —Traditional

No ear hath heard, no tongue can tell
The virtues of the Pimpernel.

> —Traditional

If the sage bush thrives and grows
The master's not master, and he knows.

> —Traditional

The Lord is Holly, and is Oak
Two sides of one—so say our folk.
The Oak lord goes, the Holly stays,
To help us through the winter days.

> —Paddy Slade, traditional English Wise Woman.

Hang an ash bough over the door
Fill your pockets with iron nails
Carry always a leaf of mullein.
　　　—Paddy Slade; blessing for the threshold.

If you wish to always have money to carry
Place in your purse three leaves of
Bergamot, bistort, and blackberry.
　　　—Traditional charm for prosperity.

BISTORT

Rue to have
Rue to hold
Rue's protection
Is often told.
　　　—Traditional

Rosemary wreath to encircle our home,
Give us fragrance, protection and light
From the mucklemark steppers
Who lurk and roam
Over hills in the dark of night.
　　　—Traditional

LAUREL

A Wedding, a woo, a clog and a shoe,
A pot of pease porridge and away they go.
    —Traditional good luck charm for newlyweds.

Laurel tree, Laurel tree,
Keep house and field lightning free.
    —Traditional

Good Morning Missus and Master,
I wish you a happy day.
Please come smell my garland
Because it is the first of May.
    —Traditional

Arm-pit package of Columba, the kindly
Unsought by me, unlooked for
I shall not be carried away in my sleep
Neither shall I be pierced with iron
Better reward of its virtues
Than a herd of cattle.
> —Traditional charm to recite when accidentally
> coming across St. Johnswort—tuck a sprig
> under your arm like St. Columba.

Coal found under the root of mugwort on
Midsummer's noon
Will keep you safe from lightning, ague
Plague and carbuncles to boot.
> —Traditional

Good Day to you, you merry men all.
Come listen to our rhyme.
For we would not have you forget
This is Midsummer time
So bring your rushes, bring your garlands,
Roses, Johnswort, Vervain, too.
Now is time for our rejoicing.
Come along Christians, come along do.
> —18th century song

I went sunways 'round my dwelling
In the name of Mother Mary
Who promised to preserve me
Who did protect me
Who will preserve me
In peace, in flocks, in righteous heart.
>   —Traditional Scottish charm to be recited at
>   Lammas in August. Shape the newest grains
>   into a stick and toast it with rowan.

Rowan tree and red thread
Hold witches in all dread.
>   —Traditional

September, blow soft
Til fruit's in the loft.
>   —Traditional

O, and I was a damsel so fair,
But fairer I wished to appear,
So I washed me in milk and I
Dressed me in silk
And put sweet thyme in my hair.
          —Devonshire song

Set garlic and beans
at St. Edmund's the King
The moon in the wane
thereof hangeth a thing.
          —Traditional charm to say in November.

Nettles grow in an angry bush
An angry bush, an angry bush,
Nettles grow in an angry bush,
With my High Ho Hum!
          —Traditional warning

Hitty Pitty within the wall
Hitty Pitty without the wall
If you touch Hitty Pitty
Hitty Pitty will bite you.
          —Traditional warning against nettles,
          or "hitty pitty."

Three blew beans in a blew bladder.
Rattle, bladder, rattle.
          —Traditional charm to keep away evil spirits.

Wassal, Wassal to our town!
The cup is white, the ale is brown.
The cup is made of ashen tree
And so is the ale of the good barley.
Little maid, little maid, turn the pin
Open the door and let us come in.
God be here. God be here.
I wish you all a Happy New Year.

   —Traditional song sung by children on
   New Year's Day.

Lavender's blue, dilly dilly
Lavender's green
When I am king, dilly dilly
You shall be queen.

   —Traditional charm sung at the Twelfth Night
   festival to choose a king and queen for good
   luck the whole year.

God have your soul
Beans and all.

   —Traditional charm recited on All Hallow's Eve
   when oat or bean cakes were given to the poor.

CHAPTER FIVE

Herbal Healing Charms

Herbal healing charms invoke the spirits of plants to keep us healthy. Many of our ancestors successfully used herbs to heal, not needing the scientific concepts behind their work. They used herbs in physical applications, as well as psychological ones.

Gathered in rural England in 1859, the five traditional rules of herbal healing charms are as follows:

1. The person to be healed must first believe.

2. The charmer and charmee must never use the words "please" or "thank you."

3. If once disclosed, the charm will lose its effectiveness.

4. The charm must be passed from mother to daughter on dying lips.

5. Offer of remuneration will break the charm.

Nettle out, Dock in.
Dock remove the nettle sting.
    —Traditional charm to cure nettle sting.

In dock, out nettle.
Don't let the blood settle.
    —Traditional

Ashen tree, ashen tree
Pray buy these warts from me.
    —Traditional charm for removing warts.

As this bean shall rot away
So my warts shall soon decay.
    —To be recited after touching the wart with a
bean; then bury the bean.

Those who would live alway
Must eat sage in May.
    —Traditional

Rue, Rue, Pure and True
Cleansing powers I claim of you:
That (name) may no longer be
Suffering from their malady.
    —Paddy Slade; charm to say while picking rue
with your left hand on a night with a full moon.

If they would eat Leeks in March
And Mugworts in May
So many young maidens wouldn't
Go to the clay.
     —Traditional

There came three angels out of the East
One brought fire, two brought frost,
Out fire, in frost.
     —Traditional charm to treat a burn; apply
     blackberry leaves and recite.

The Maiden Bride came out of the East.
     —Traditional charm to heal a scald: take nine
     blackberry leaves and dip them in spring water.
     Lay against the wound and say three times to
     each leaf.

Round and green, hen and chick
Sting of burns allay
Rosy leaves will stick and prick
But keep lightning away.
     —Traditional charm, "hen and chick" is
     the herb sedum.

Tobacco hic
Will make you well
If you be sick.
     —Traditional, when tobacco was considered
     medicinal.

Regimen ſanitatis

Dis iſt ein Regiment der geſuntheit durch
alle Monadt des gantzen Jares/wie
man ſich halté ſol mit eſſen vnd
auch mit trincken vñ ſaget
auch von aderlaſſen.

This month thou mayest Physicke take
And bleed and bathe for thy health's sake.
Eat figs and grapes and spicery
For to refresh thy members dry.
    —Neve's Almanac, 17th century advice for the
    month of September.

Unto Virgin Mary our Saviour was born.
And on his head he wore a crown of thorn.
If you believe this true and mind it well
This hurt will never fester and swell.
    —Traditional charm for a thorn.

Although the words have been long forgotten, a traditional healing charm was made with the following herbs: fennel, balm, pine, savory, mint, columbine, parsley, basil and thyme.

CHAPTER SIX

Tree Charms

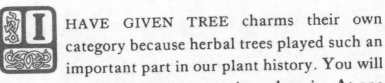

I HAVE GIVEN TREE charms their own category because herbal trees played such an important part in our plant history. You will hear rhymes relating to trees again and again. At one time our calendar was based on the lunar cycles, each of which was named for a tree.

Old Gal, give me some of your wood,
And when I am a tree, I will give you some of mine.
   —Traditional charm recited when cutting a tree.

When nights and days are balanced and halved
Cut from the branches March has saved
Twelve supple wands all budded green
Twist together to weave a crown.
   —Paddy Slade

The Maypole is up.
Now give me the cup.
I'll drink to the garlands around it.
Be first to those
Whose hands did compose
The glory of the flowers that crown'd it.
　　—Traditional song recorded in 1657.

Nut for a slut
Plum for the glum.
Bramble for she who is a ramble.
Gorse for whores.
　　—Traditional insults said when May Day
　　greenery is hung at someone's door.

Oak and May
Upon this day
Will both heed
Those in need.
　　—Traditional May Day charm.

Hang the leaf from a sturdy limb
Of Oak or Maple or Ash or Elm
Thus will the tree live long and well.
　　—Paddy Slade

Burn ash new, burn ash old
Is fit for a queen with a crown of gold.
    —Traditional

Fairy folks
Are in old Oaks.
    —Traditional

Beechwood fires burn bright and clear
If logs be kept a year.
Oaken logs if dry and old
Keep away the winter's cold.
Chestnut's only good, they say,
If for years tis laid away.
But ashwood green or ashwood brown
Are fit for a king with a golden crown.
Elm, she burns like churchyard mould.
Even the flames are very cold.
Birch and pine wood burn too fast.
Blaze too bright and do not last.
But ash wet or ash dry
A queen may warm her slippers by.
      —Traditional instructional charm
      for burning wood.

Pippin pippin fly away
Give me one another day.
      —Traditional charm recited while eating an
      apple and spitting seeds.

Stand fast root, bear well top.
God send us a youling sop.
Every twig, apple big.
Every bough, apples enow.
Hats full, caps full,
Full quarter sacks full.

—"Youling" is the custom of blessing fruits of the coming year. The name may come from Eolus, ancient god of the wind. Young men circled fruit trees and pronounced this charm. They expected money or a drink from the tree's owner.

Love Charms and Herbal Divinations

THE LOVE CHARMS were typically only for girls, since—in the recent and distant past—marriage was usually a female's only acceptable fate. A woman's future was tied with her mate's, usually through no choice of her own. As his life went, so went hers. A woman could rarely choose to pursue an individual livelihood, and could never ask a man to marry her!

Yarrow, sweet yarrow, the first I have found.
In the name of the Lord, I pluck thee
     from the ground.
As the Lord loves the Lady, so warm and dear,
So in my dream may my lover appear.
     —Traditional

Ivy, Ivy, I love you
in my bosom I put you.
The first young man to speak to me
My future husband he shall be.
—Traditional

If (name) loves me, pop and fly.
If (name) hates me, burn and die.
—Traditional hazel nut charm for the hearth.

Even ash, even ash, I pluck thee off the tree.
The first man I meet, my true love he be.
—Traditional

Of violets and lavender, take a few
Enclose them with myrtle of dark green hue
Make them in a posy, small and round and bright
You may see your true love in your
dreams tonight.
—Paddy Slade

Thou silver glow-worm, lend me thy light
I must gather St. Johnswort herb this night
The wonderful herb whose leaf does decide
If the coming year shall make me a bride.
　　—Traditional love charm, said when gathering
　　St. Johnswort leaves very early on
　　Midsummer's Day.

By a prophetic rose leaf I found
Your changed affection, for it gave no sound.
Though in my hand struck hollow as it lay,
But quickly withered, like your love, away.
　　—Traditional love charm to recite when laying a
　　rose petal in your left hand, and hitting it with
　　your right fist. If it pops, your lover loves you, if
　　it is quiet, he does not.

Titsy Totsy, tell me true
Who shall I be married to?
　　—A charm using cowslips to string flowers to
　　make a "cucking ball." Throw from one girl to
　　another, calling a maiden and a bachelor's name
　　with each throw. When the ball is dropped, that
　　girl and man will marry.

If you find an ash leaf and a four-leaved clover
You'll see your true love ere the day be over.
    —Traditional

Green yarrow, green yarrow, you bears
   white blow
If my love loves me my nose will bleed now.
    —Charm recited while yarrow leaves are pushed
    up the nostrils.

The even-ash leaf in my hand,
The first I meet shall be my man.
    —Traditional

A Clover, a clover of two
put it in your right shoe.
The first man you meet in field, land or street,
You'll have him or one of his name.
    —Traditional charm with a two-leaved clover.

Hempseed I sow, hempseed I throw,
Let him who be my true love come after me now.
>—Charm recited one half hour before bedtime
>while scattering hemp seed.

Rosemary for remembrance between us day and night
Wishing I may always have you present in my sight.
>—Love charm to bind a lover to you. To be
>recited after giving lover a sprig of rosemary.

A fair maid, who the first of May
Goes to the fields at the break of day
And washes in dew from the Hawthorne
Will ever after handsome be.
>—Traditional

Good St. Faith, be kind tonight
And bring to me my heart's delight.
Let me my future husband view
And be my vision chaste and true.
>—Traditional charm, recited while eating cake
>made with spring water and rosemary. Cut it
>into 9 pieces and pass it through a wedding ring
>of a woman married 7 years, then eat the cake
>and recite.

St. Valentine, be kind to me.
In dreams let me my true love see.
> —Traditional love charm to be recited while
> laying bay leaves sprinkled with rosewater on
> your pillow before bedtime.

I offer this my sacrifice
To him most precious in my eyes.
I charge thee now come forth to me,
That I this minute may thee see.
> —Two young women sit together in a darkened
> room from midnight until 1 a.m. They take as
> many hairs as they are old out of their heads
> and put in a linen cloth with the herb "truelove"
> (rosemary). When the clock strikes 1, each must
> burn the hairs separately, reciting the charm, at
> which time the future husbands will appear,
> walk around the room, and disappear. Neither
> girl will see the other's lover.

Kernel come kernel, hop over my thumb.
And tell me which way my true love will come.
East, West, North or South
Kernel jump into my true love's mouth.
> —A rare love divination for boys. They must
> shoot a seed or kernel with their thumbs while
> reciting the charm.

Good St. Thomas do me right
And let my true love come tonight
That I may see him in the face
And him in my kind arms embrace.
      —Peel an onion, wrap it up in a clean
      handkerchief, placing it under your pillow before
      bed while reciting the charm.

Roses are red
Violets are blue
Pinks are sweet
And so are you.
      —It was customary to
      draw lots for a love at St.
      Valentine's Day. Many
      marriage arrangements
      were actually made at this
      time.

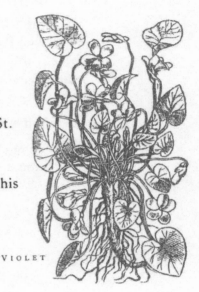

VIOLET

This even-ash I double three
The first man I meet my true love will be.
If he be married let him pass by,
But if he be single, let him draw nigh.
      —Traditional charm recited while a girl held ash
      leaves with an even number of leaflets in her
      hand.

If your love to you you'd bring
Hold these in your hand in Spring.
Myrtle green and violets blue,
Then will your love come to you.
    —Paddy Slade

Fire sweet and fire red
Warm the heart and turn the head.
    —Pick your red and green apple when the moon
    has waned three days. Breathe upon the green
    cheek, rubbing it with a scarlet cloth while
    reciting charm.

Kiss the red half of the apple, put it in another's hand.
Who holds it shall weaken, who eats it will be yours.
    —Traditional

Come, sweetheart come,
Dear as my heart to me.
Come into the room
I have made for thee.
Flowers for thee to tread.
Green herbs, sweet scented.
    —Traditional 10th century love song.

In **Herbal Divination Charms,** plants were called upon to help us find satisfying answers to troubling questions. Sometimes they warned us of particular activities.

Sweep with a broom
That is cut in May.
You'll sweep the head
Of the house away.
    —Traditional

If on the 8th of June it rain,
Then foretells a wet harvest, men sayen.
    —Traditional

St. Mathews Day, bright and clear
Brings good wine in next year.
    —Traditional charm, for when Autumnal
    equinox falls on St. Mathews Day.

A seed-case full of wisdom and grace
Inside your head my question I place.
Beneath my pillow through the night,
I shall dream the answer right.
    —Paddy Slade. Your question is to be written in
    blue ink on white paper and placed inside a
    poppy seed pod, while reciting the charm.

Onion skin, very thin,
Mild Winter's coming in.
Onion skin, thick and tough,
Coming winter cold and rough.
    —Traditional

Sow in the sop,
Twill be heavy a-top.
    —Traditional charm for seeds sown in wet
    weather.

Herbal Charms for Plant Protection

HERBAL CHARMS FOR plant protection refer to the critical value of the garden itself. We invoke plants and herbs themselves to help us with favorable weather and gardening.

And thou, Waybrood!
Mother of Worts
Open from eastward
Mighty within
Over thee carts creaked
Over thee queens rose
Over thee brides bridalled
Over thee bulls threathed
All these thou withstood'st
Venom and all vile things
And loathely ones
That through the land rove
—Charm to praise plantain, or waybrood, from 11th century manuscript written by the monk Aelfic.

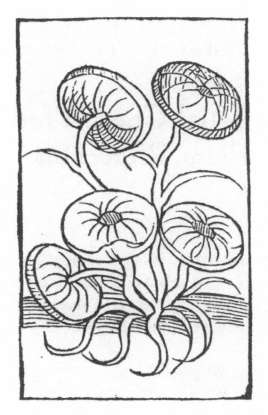

When the Moon is at the full,
Mushrooms you may freely pull;
But when the moon is on the wane,
Wait were you to think to pluck again.
    —Traditional

Summer Summer Savory
I need you for my beans
I plant when moon is havery
with marigolds in between.
    —Paddy Slade

Malum Depuo, Hostem Veneno Caedo Caedo, or
Evil enemy, I prune, I poison, I cut into pieces.
   —Charm against weeds in the garden. Under a
   waning moon, break one leaf from the garden's
   tallest weed. Crush it with your teeth, spitting
   the fragments upon the earth while reciting the
   charm. Next, cut off the stalk with a silver
   knife, and spread a handful of salt over the
   hidden root.

One for the rook, one for the crow,
One to die and one to grow.
    —Traditional seed-sowing charm.

Sowe peason and beans, in the wane of the moon,
Who soweth them sooner, he soweth too soone.
    —Traditional

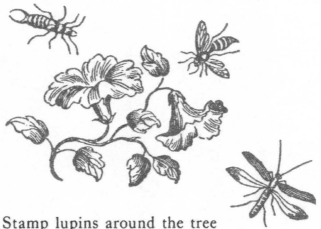

Stamp lupins around the tree
From ants and pismires it will be free.
    —Traditional

More in the garden grows
Than the gardener knows.
    —Traditional

Yarrow, yarrow tremble and sway
Tiny flowers bright and gay
Protect my garden night and day.
    —Traditional

When Elmen leaves are big as a shilling,
Plant kidney beans if you mean to have any.
When Elmen leaves are big as a penny,
Plant kidney beans if you mean to have any.
When Elmen leaves is as big as an ox's eye,
Then say I, "Hi boys, Hi."
    —Traditional

The Blessed Virgin Maries feast hath here her
    place and time
Wherin departing from the earth, she did the
    heavens chime
Great bundels then of hearbes to church the
    people fast do bear
To which against all hurtful things the priest do
    hallow there.
    —16th century song to bless herbs and plants.

If you set it
The cats will get it.
If you sow it
The cat's won't know it.
　　　—Traditional catnip charm

As we redyn, gaderyd most hym be
With iii pater-noster and iii ave,
Fastand, thou the wedire be grylle,
Be-twen mydde March and mydde Aprille,
And set awysyd most the bo,
That the sonne be in ariete.
　　　—14th century charm on the virtues of herbs.

All hele, thou holy herb vervain,
Growing on the ground.
In the mount of Calvary
There was thou found.
Thou helpst many a griefe,
And stenchest many a wound.
In the name of Jesus,
I take thee from the ground.
O Lord, effect the same
That I doe now goe about.
　　　—15th century rhyme from manuscript in
　　　Manchester to be said while gathering vervain.

In the name of God, on Mt. Olivet
First I thee found.
In the name of Jesus
I pull thee from the ground.

> —Traditional charm to recite while gathering
> vervain.

CHAPTER NINE

Herbal Fairy Charms

HERBAL FAIRY CHARMS are some of the oldest recorded rhymes. They have nearly passed out of our oral tradition altogether since today only children believe in fairies. An old adage is that fairies always talk in rhyme. Let's hope these old charms can bring the fairies back into all of our gardens!

Fairies dance near thyme
Under the moon in June.
    —Traditional

Fairy folks
Are in old oaks.
    —Traditional

[79]

Thyme and thyme and thyme again
Help us dance like fairies can.
—Traditional

Fairy bells (woodsorrel)
Fairy cheese (mallow)
Fairy cap (foxglove)
Fairy flax (groundflax)
Fairy horse (ragwort)
Fairy tables (toadstools)
Fairy cups (primroses)
—Traditional charm for a fairy garland. To see
the fairies, wear the garland and repeat the
names three times.

A pint of sallet oyle and put in a vial glass; and
first wash it with rose-water; the flowers to be
gathered towards the east, wash it til the oyle
becomes white, then put thereto the budds of
hollyhocks, the flowers of marygolde, the
flowers of toppes of wild thyme, the budds of
young hazle, and the thyme must be gathered
near the side of a hill where fairies used to be;
and take grasse of a fairy throne; then all these
put into the glass and set it to dissolve three
days in the sunne and keep it for thy use.
—From a manuscript in the Ashmolean
Museum in Oxford, England.

A Compendium of
Magical Herbs

 grimony *(Agrimonia eupatoria)* If agrimony is placed under a sleeping man's head, he will not awaken until it is removed.

Angelica *(Angelica archangelica)* Angelica is believed to have a heavenly origin. Poets made crowns of it for inspiration. Roots of the herb hung around the neck will protect against evil and enchantment.

Anise *(Pimpinella anisum)* The seeds of anise avert the evil eye.

Apple *(Malus)* It is the sacred fruit of the Celts. The mythological holy land was Avalon, Isle of Apples. Fairy tales and religious stories are filled with the magic of apples. Many love charms use apples for conjuring up a lover.

Ash *(Fraxinus)* If you carry an ash twig, you will be safe.

Aspen *(Populus)* It is the symbol of talkativeness. If aspen is laid upon a sorcerer's grave, it will ensure the soul stays earth-bound.

Basil *(Ocimum basilicum)* It is the most sacred herb in India. Sweethearts in western cultures give leaves of basil as symbols of love. Its leaves left under a pot will turn into a scorpion. The seeds will not germinate unless sown with verbal abuse.

Bay *(Laurus nobilis)* The Greeks dedicated it to Apollo, and viewed it as a symbol of the sun's powers. In Rome, bay was the symbol of victory. It is always paired with rosemary at weddings and funerals. It offers protection from lightning, thunder, witches, and devils.

Bee balm *(Monarda didyma)* This herb was traditionally carried to church where it received its other name, bibleleaf.

Betony *(Pedicularis)* It offers such great protection from water snakes and kelpies (Scottish water spirits) that the old saying is, "Sell your coat and buy betony."

Birch *(Betula)* A twig given to a woman by a man signifies a romantic interest. Twigs made into a broom sweep away evil spirits.

Blackberry *(Rubus)* The magical associations with the blackberry are often the same as for the grapevine. It is bad luck to eat blackberries after the September feast of St. Michael, when the devil spits on them.

Blackthorn *(Crataegus)* This is the tree of both black magic and wisdom. Sorcerers made their walking sticks of blackthorn.

Borage *(Borago officinalis)* This herb imparts courage to those who carry it, or drink tea or ale in which it has been steeped. "I Borage give Courage" is the ancient phrase of renown. The herb also encourages cheerfulness. It was traditionally used to decorate houses for weddings.

Caraway *(Carum carvi)* The seeds prevent theft of any object containing them. A straying husband will come home if his wife slips caraway seeds in his pocket.

Carnation *(Dianthus caryophyllus)* Also known as clove gillyflowers, this herb is the symbol of gentleness. It will fade if the master or mistress of the house dies.

Catnip *(Nepeta cataria)* This herb attracts cats and repels rats.

CHAMOMILE

Chamomile *(Anthemis nobilis)* Early herbalists recommended it to drive away nightmares. Chamomile represents the ability to bounce back after adversity.

Chervil *(Anthriscus cerefolium)* Herbalist Gerard insisted chervil "provoketh lust." It is said to restore youth, and to cure the hiccups.

Chives *(Allium schoenoprasum)* Chives have a lineage of over 5000 years. A plant sacred to ancient Egyptians, chives are pictured on their monuments. King Oberon's elfin troupe puff on tiny pipes made of hollow chive stems, and gypsies tell fortunes with the dried stalks.

Clover *(Trifolium)* Four-leaved clovers will enable the bearer to see fairies, and to avoid military service.

Comfrey *(Symphytum officinale)* Its common name is knitbone. Its renowned power is to knit together meat boiling in a pot.

CORIANDER

Coriander *(Coriandrum sativum)* In the Bible it was called manna, the magical food. It is used as an aphrodisiac and to conjure up evil spirits.

Costmary *(Tanacetum balsamita)* Like bee balm, this herb is sometimes called bibleleaf because it was carried to church, often dried to make a bookmark.

Dock *(Rumex)* These stalks are able to strike down enemies.

Elder *(Alnus glutinosa)* This is a magical herbal tree. There is an elder tree mother who lives in each elder tree and watches over it. Before cutting an elder tree, always ask permission, or bad luck will follow. If you stand near an elder tree on Midsummer's Eve, you will see Toly, King of the Elves, and his procession.

Elecampane *(Inula helenium)* This huge plant is said to have been held by Helen of Troy as she was born away by Paris. Its common name is "elfdock," and it attracts fairies.

Elm *(Ulmaceae)* This tree is especially loved by fairies and elves. It also protects from lightning.

Endive *(Cichorium intybus)* This is one of the most well-known herbal aphrodisiacs. The seeds are used in love potions.

Fennel *(Foeniculum vulgare)* In an earlier age than ours, it was said to restore lost vision. "Fennel is for flatterers" is the old adage. It is the symbol of success; when hung in homes it will discourage evil. It was used by sorcerers to conjure up evil spirits.

Fern *(Ophioglossum vulgatum)* Fernseed carried in a pocket will make you invisible.

Feverfew *(Chrysanthemum parthenium)* It carries the folk name of bridesbutton. Our foremothers carried it in their bridal bouquets. It will cleanse the air, ward off disease, and purge a siege of melancholy. Feverfew in the garden will entice fairies to dance there.

Flax *(Linum)* This herb is especially loved by Hulda, the Teutonic goddess who taught mortals how to spin and weave. Children who dance in the flax flowers are beautiful and have supernatural skills.

Foxglove *(Digitalis)* This plant should always be gathered with the left hand from the north side.

Garlic *(Allium liliaeae)* This herb is the most potent folk symbol against evil. Sacred to the ancient Greeks and Egyptians, garlic was said to have sprung up from the footprint of the devil.

Germander *(Teucrium lucidum)* This herb strengthens the brain and helps overcome apprehension.

Good King Henry *(Chenopodium Bonus Henricus)* This herb is appropriated to Heinrich, the Teutonic household goblin who plays tricks, or helps with the housework. Heinrich asks only for a bowl of cream and this herb to be set out at night for him.

Hare Thistle *(Sonchus oleraceus)* In the old herbals, this plant is described as protecting rabbits from predators.

Hawthorn *(Crataegus oxyacantha)* This traditional hedgerow tree is known for its protection from bad luck and mischievous spirits. It is the symbol of female sovereignty. If you wantonly cut down a hawthorn tree, bad luck will befall your children and your cattle.

Hazel *(Corylus)* A twig given by a woman to a man signifies romance.

Hellebore *(Helleborus niger)* It is known as the Christmas rose or bearsfoot. Country people use it to protect their cattle. To harvest it: draw a magic circle around it with a sword, turn to the east, and ask Apollo and Aesculapius for permission to dig up the root. A sorcerer can pass invisibly if he scatters the hellebore seed before him. One of its bifurcated leaves is evil, but only a witch can tell which.

Hemlock *(Cicutaria palustris)* Water hemlock is a poisonous herb used to subdue lust. Evergreen hemlock *(Conium maculatum)* is grown in cemeteries and around homes to protect from evil.

Henbane *(Hyoseyamus niger)* More poisonous than magical, henbane is gathered with great care and ritual.

Hens and chicks *(Sedum)* This herb gives protection from evil and mischance. Its folk names are fascinating: Jupiter's Beard, old man and old woman, stonecrop, wall pepper, senegrene, and welcome-home-husband-though-never-so-drunk, as well as others. It will protect a home from lightning when grown in the garden or on a wall. It was included in an old charm by Albertus Magnus, a 15th century German writer, to catch fish . . . *de virtubibus herbarum animalium et mirabilis mundi.*

Holly *(Ilex)* This evergreen is associated with Midwinter festivals, and represents the male element. It is hung for good luck because it survives when even the mighty oak loses its leaves in winter.

Holy Thistle *(Carduus Benedictus)* This herb is dedicated to Thor and used as protection against lightning. A charm against the plague includes holy thistle; it also cures melancholy. A cure to an open wound calls for placing four thistles at four points of the compass with a stone in the center.

Honesty *(Lunaria)* This herb brings prosperity to those who grow it in the garden, but only an honest person can make it thrive. It will also pull the shoes off a horse that is ridden over it.

Honeysuckle *(Lonicera)* The scent of this twining vine is known as an aphrodisiac. Parents forbid young girls from sleeping in a room with honeysuckle, because it will inspire lustful dreams.

Hops *(Humulus lupulus)* Hops flowers will make you fall asleep and have pleasant dreams.

Horehound *(Marrubium vulgare)* The old herbalists praised it for bringing good luck and curing a cough. Ancient Egyptians called it the "Seed of Horus," saying that it will protect one from the bite of a dog.

HOREHOUND

Hound's Tongue *(Cynoglossum officinale)* This herb has the property of preventing dogs from barking if a leaf is laid in your shoe or sprinkled about.

Hyssop *(Hyssopus officinalis)* This is the traditional herb of cleansing and purification. Newlyweds hang it in their houses, as do housewives after a thorough cleaning. It is hated by evil spirits.

Ivy *(Hedera helix)* This twining evergreen represents the female element. Its leaves have five points, a number sacred to the earth goddess. Ivy symbolizes retirement, concealment, and protection. It is also thought to prevent drunkenness. Therefore, ivy is often seen on tavern signs or around the punch bowl.

Juniper *(Juniperus communis)* This tree has long been regarded as magical against devils, evil spirits, and dangerous wild animals.

LADY'S MANTLE

Lady's Mantle *(Alchemilla vulgaris)* This herb is dedicated to the Virgin Mary. If a girl-child's face is washed each morning in the dew that collects on a lady's mantle leaf, she will grow up to be a beautiful and powerful woman. Dawn is the hour at which the dew is most magical.

Lady's Smock *(Cardimine pratensis)* This herb is dedicated to the Virgin Mary; it is used to call upon her protection. The old herbalists used it to deck up the garlands of country people.

Lavender *(Lavandula officinalis)* Lavender is the symbol of truth and purity. Lavender flowers quilted in a cap comfort the brain. Strewn in churches on holy days, lavender is also thrown into bonfires on Midsummer's Eve. In Italy, it protects children from the evil eye.

Leeks *(Allium porrum)* This large flat-leaved onion is sacred to the Welsh. Eaten in the Spring, leeks ensure good luck throughout the year.

Lemon balm *(Melissa officinalis)* This is the consoling herb. It has the virtue of bouncing back after every mishap, and has the same influence on those around it. It is an important strewing herb, especially at bridal feasts. A 13th century wedding recalls "nine baskets of balme, two women to a basket, each basket containing two bushels of herbs." *Brand's Popular Antiquities.*

Lettuce *(Lactuca)* Lettuce will cause you to fall asleep. It is bad luck to eat lettuce in hot weather.

Lovage *(Ligusticum officinale)* This herb is dedicated to the sun.

Mandrake *(Mandragora officinarum)* The old belief surrounding this herb is that mandrake shrieked like a human when pulled from the ground. Elaborate rituals were used to harvest it. It is an aphrodisiac and encourages fertility.

Marchwort *(Somoclas)* This is a strange little herb once put into watering troughs to strengthen horses and cattle. To be harvested properly, it must be cut while fasting,  with the left hand, without looking backward.

Marigolds *(Calendula)* This pretty flower is sometimes called the mistress of all flowers on earth. It is also called golds and calendula. Dedicated to the Virgin Mary, marigolds represent shields carried into battle. They are also the symbol of jealousy. Dreaming of marigolds foretells of wealth, success, and a rich and happy marriage. To gather calendulas, one must be free of deadly sin, and recite three Pater Nosters and three Ave Marias.

Marjoram *(Origanum)* This is the gypsy herb of romance. Houses are traditionally decorated with marjoram for weddings. Children are told if they sniff marjoram their noses will fall off.

Meadowsweet *(Spiraea ulmaria)* Queen-of-the-meadow and brideswort are two folk names for this herb. Old herbalists say its smell makes the heart merry and delights the senses. It is a favorite decorating and strewing herb. When meadowsweet is thrown into a pool on Midsummer's Eve, it will help to reveal a thief. If it sinks, the thief is a man; if it floats, the thief is a woman.

MARJORAM

Mint *(Mentha)* In mythology Mintha was a beautiful nymph who loved Pluto, god of the underworld. In a jealous rage, Persephone changed her into the little mint plant. Mint still grows in dark, damp places. It is an important strewing herb described as "causing the rejoiceth of the heart." Mint's scent relaxes the nerves, stimulates the brain, and causes lustful dreams in the night.

Mistletoe *(Phoradendron serotinum)* When found growing in the top of an oak or apple tree, mistletoe must be cut with a golden sickle and dropped upon a white cloth—never the ground. Mistletoe is most magical when found growing on a hawthorn. When hanging mistletoe at Christmas time, one should use whole bunches, not just small twigs. It is considered a powerful aphrodisiac (hence kissing beneath it), therefore called "all heal." An old recipe for a cure called for: "as much mistletoe as would lie on a sixpence early in the morning in black-cherry water or beer, for a few days near the full moon."

Monkshood *(Aconitum napellus)* Also known as wolfbane, this pretty (but highly poisonous) herb was used on the tips of paralyzing arrows. Elfbolt is its other common name.

Moonwort *(Botrychium lunaria)* This herb has another country name: unshoe-the-horse. Supposedly it will pull the shoes off any horse which passes over it.

Mugwort *(Artemisia vulgaris)* This may be the most magical herb of all! Putting a sprig in one's shoe prevents weariness. Placing a sprig in one's shoe on Midsummer's Eve will cause you to be carried about on a white horse. At daylight, the horse will disappear, leaving you stranded.

Nightshade *(Atropa belladonna)* Deadly nightshade is to be avoided at all costs. The adage says she appears as a beautiful woman by the side of the road.

Oak *(Quercus)* This tree is an ancient symbol of strength and protection. It is the most sacred to Celts, and its leaf is often used as an emblem. The line "Hey, Derry Down," often heard in folksongs, is a corruption of early language, meaning "In a wide circle, oak tree move around."

Oregano *(Origanum vulgare)* This is another of the strewing herbs. It is used in washing waters and is a symbol of honor.

Pansies *(Viola)* Hearts-ease, Johnny-jump-up, and tri-colored violet are all types of pansies. They are cherished as provoking thought and cheerfulness. To be irresistible, you should bathe in goat's milk and violet flowers.

Parsley *(Petroselinum crispum)* Never transplant parsley or bad luck will come. The seeds are said to go to the devil and back nine times before they will germinate. Traditionally, to plant parsley meant a death would come to the family within the year. Therefore, seeds were often placed so the wind would sow them. Parsley was often planted on graves. An old saying meaning one is at death's door is, "He is in great need of parsley." Ancient Greeks, however, used parsley for athletic victory garlands.

Peas *(Fabaceae)* Wearing pea blossoms will attract lovers.

Pennyroyal *(Mentha pulegium)* It is traditionally put in the crèche at Christmas because it will burst into bloom at midnight. In Italy it is protection against the evil eye. When warring spouses offer one another sprigs of pennyroyal, peace will prevail.

Peony *(Paeonia)* This herb is known to dispel tempests. It will also release you from enchantments. Seeds gathered at the waning of the moon and hung around the necks of children are good against hauntings, fairies, and witches. If a woodpecker is in sight when peony is gathered, the gatherer will go blind.

Periwinkle *(Vinca)* This herb's French name is *violette de sorcier*. The Italians call it the flower of the dead. The Germans call it the flower of immortality. A traditional aphrodisiac recipe calls for periwinkle, houseleeks, and earthworms. Periwinkle leaves eaten by a man and a woman together will cause love between them.

Pimpernel *(Anagallis arvensis)* This plant protects against enchantments.

Plantain *(Plantago major)* This plant was once a maiden waiting for her lover by the side of the road. At last she changed into plantain and only once a year becomes a bird for a day. Plantain is a symbol of loyalty. An old saying about plantain reads: "As true as Plantago to the moon."

Poppy *(Papaver somniferum)* Although the foliage is used medicinally, the seeds are emblems of good fortune.

Primrose *(Primula)* Puck's face is often seen peeking out of the primrose blossom. Its petals are used to see if a lover is in fact in love. It is an ancient restorer of lost beauty.

PRIMROSE

Purslane *(Portulaca)* Strewn about a bed, it offers protection from evil spirits. It is also good against the blastings of lightning and planets.

Radish *(Raphanus sativus)* No snake will approach if you carry a radish in your pocket.

Ragwort *(Senecio)* Also known as St. Jameswort, ragwort is the herb of horses. Witches ride on its stems, giving it the name witches' horse. In Ireland fairies ride it, calling it fairy horse. It is especially loved by leprechauns or clauricanes (fairy cobblers). Every leprechaun has a hidden treasure under a ragwort.

Ramps *(Allium tricoccum)* Always grown in the magician's garden, ramps are used in magic spells. In Italy they excite quarrels.

Reed *(Phragmites communis)* This plant is associated with royalty and music. It also symbolizes letting the spirits of the living and the dead fly freely.

Rose *(Rosa)* This is the queen of flowers. Associated with Venus and Aphrodite, the rose is the flower of women. Flora, the Goddess of Flowers, was overcome by the death of her favorite nymph, and implored all the other gods and goddesses to turn her immortal essence into a mortal flower. Apollo gave the rose the power of the sun; Bacchus bathed it in nectar; and Flora gave it beauty and color.

Rosemary *(Rosmarinus)* Rosemary is the symbol of friendship, love and remembrance. Although it is dedicated to the Virgin Mary, it was cherished long before Christianity. It is customary to distribute rosemary sprigs to mourners at funerals and to drop the sprigs into the grave. Judges will sometimes put rosemary on the dock at court to comfort the heart and help a weak memory. Rosemary dipped in scented water was carried at weddings as a sign of wisdom, love, and loyalty. In 1603, Mr. Decker wrote

> Here is a strange alteration, for the Rosemary that was washt in sweet water to set out the Bridall, is now wet in Teares to furnish her Buriall.
> —*Brand's Popular Antiquities*

Rowan *(Sorbus)* Also known as mountain ash, rowan is planted outside homes to protect those within from evil. Other folk names include quickbeam, wichen, witchwood, and witchbane. It is particularly useful planted outside barns to protect animals from curses. A rowan twig should always be hung above the bed. A rowan crop is the only way to control a bewitched horse.

Rue *(Ruta graveolens)* At least since the time of ancient Greece, rue has been recorded as a powerful defense against evil. In Germany bunches of rue and ground ivy enable the bearer to see elves. Rue is the English word for sorrow and remorse, but it is the herb of repentance. Sometimes called herb of grace, it is used at high mass. Rue can divine the future, and is powerful against wild beasts if hung in windows and at every door.

Saffron *(Crocus sativus)* Irish women dye their sheets with saffron to give strength to their limbs and to encourage conception.

Sage *(Salvia)* *"Cur morietur homo cui Salvia crescit in horto?"* "How can a man die who grows sage in his garden?" goes the old adage. Sage promotes a happy home. Where sage thrives, the woman rules. Toads love to sit under sage. Once upon a time, only those old and wise could use sage.

St. Johnswort *(Hypericum perforatum)* This plant is associated with the summer solstice near the feast of St. John. Used to exorcise evil spirits, St. Johnswort gives great protection. Its botanical name actually means "over an apparition" in Greek.

Savory *(Satureja montana)* The ancients believed savory was the herb of satyrs and under the dominion of Mercury. "Keep it by you all year if you love yourself and your ease, and it is a hundred pounds to a penny if you do not," is the adage.

Seaweeds *(Fucus)* Known as Lady's Trees, seaweed is dried and hung in cottages to give protection from fire and evil spirits.

Southernwood *(Artemisia abrotanum)* This herb has a long association with romance, as evidenced by its long list of folk names: Lad's Love, Old Man, Maiden's Ruin. It is always included in a country lover's bouquet. Young boys rub its ashes on their faces to grow a beard. Burning it drives away serpents.

Springwort *(Claytonia)* A lock will yield if you touch it with springwort. In Switzerland, it is carried in one's pocket to protect from dagger or bullet. In the Harz mountains of Germany, it reveals hidden treasures. To gather springwort, you must find an empty woodpecker nest and fill it with wood. When the woodpecker returns, it will bring a sprig of the herb to unstop its nest. Meanwhile, a fire must be built on a red cloth placed nearby so the bird will be frightened and drop the magical springwort.

Stitchwort *(Stellaria graminea)*
This herb must never be picked because it is the property of the elves and fairies.

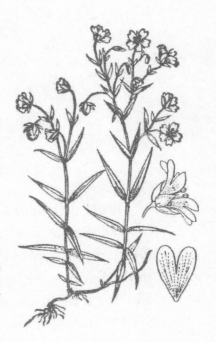

Strawberries *(Fragaria)* The waters of the berries are good for passions of the heart and to make one merry.

Sweet Marjoram *(Origanum marjorana)* This little herb is the symbol of virtue. It is used to bathe an aching head.

STITCHWORT

Sweet Woodruff *(Asperula odorata)* Used in May wine,
Sweet Woodruff is good luck for the growing season. Made into garlands and hung in the heat of summer, it tempers the air, cooling and refreshing all who are in the room.

TANSY

Tansy *(Tanacetum vulgare)* Its name comes from "Athanasia" or immortality. The herb is traditional at Easter and Passover as a bitter herb. Tansy cakes eaten in the Spring were so prized that they were given to the winning team in a hand-ball game in old England. Boys steal a girl's shoe, to be redeemed for a tansy cake. A tansy leaf in your shoe will prevent a cold, but giving a tansy leaf to someone is a great insult.

Tarragon *(Artemisia dracunculus)* This one is the "little dragon" which increases stamina by just having it near. The old legend is that the seed of flax put into a radish root or sea onion will bring forth tarragon.

Thornapple *(Datura stramonium)* Also called sorcerer's herb, this poisonous herb was once used as a love philtre.

Thyme *(Thymus)* This plant is an ancient symbol of energy and magic. Almost every old charm to see fairies includes thyme. Fairies lay their sleeping babies in thyme blossoms when they go dancing at night. To encourage the wee folk back into your garden in the Spring, set out little bowls of thyme on May Eve. Just to wear a sprig of thyme renews the spirit. Its fragrance has been called dawn in paradise.

TOBACCO

Tobacco *(Nicotiana)* Tobacco has diverse uses, including being grown as a decorative plant with fragrant white flowers. It is greatly favored by Puck, and growing it will entice the sprite into your garden.

Vervain *(Verbena officinalis)* It is crushed and worn as a charm against evil sorcerers. Legend reputes vervain was used to staunch the wounds of Christ. It is used to divine the future by looking through its blossoms to see visions of things to come.

Vine *(Vitis vinifera)* This is the old name for grapevine. The plant is associated with poets and inspiration. It is the symbol of Dionysus and the blood of Christ, both mystical and magical. Its five-pointed leaves are sacred to the Love Goddess, Aphrodite.

Viper's Bugloss *(Echium vulgare)* It has the force and virtue to drive away sorrow and pensiveness of the heart.

Wild Geranium *(Geranium maculatum)* Also known as cransebill, this pretty plant is a powerful talisman against the plague and other infectious diseases.

Willow *(Salix)* Willow trees are sacred to poets. Owned by the moon, it is the tree of the Muse and all artistic inspiration. Wearing a willow leaf now symbolizes grief over loss, but once was worn as protection from a jealous moon goddess. It is one of the most ancient symbols for women. A willow mother is said to reside in each willow tree. The words wicker and witch are derived from the word willow.

Witch Hazel *(Hamamelis)* The wood of the witch hazel is used to divine the future and to douse for water.

Wormwood *(Artemisia absinthium)* Like all the artemisias, it is named after the moon goddess, Diana, who found them and delivered their powers to mortals. According to the ancients, it counteracts the effects of poisoning by toadstools, hemlock, shrews, and dragons. It also draws down the power of the moon.

Yarrow *(Achillea millefolium)* This decorative herb is used for conjuring and to detect sorcerers. It will tremble when one with evil intentions comes near it. It is used in many good luck and love charms.

Yew *(Taxaceae)* This tree offers powerful protection. It is traditionally grown on the southwest side of the home. The fruit and needles of the evergreen are poisonous to ingest. Legend says you will become invisible if you hide in a yew tree.

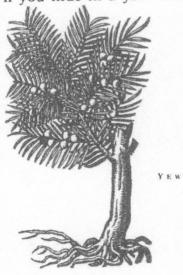

YEW

You must observe Mother Bumbies rules to take just so many knots or sprigs and no more, lest fall out that it do you no good, if you catch no harme by it.

—Traditional 17th century charm.

ABOUT THE AUTHOR

LINDA OURS RAGO tends her dooryard herb garden beside her early 19th century brick house. In this house she and her husband reared their family in Harpers Ferry, West Virginia.

Linda gathers wild herbs from around a mountain cabin at Blackberry Cove in Hampshire County, West Virginia, where her family first settled in 1753.

A long standing member of the Herb Society of America, the author has also written *Dooryard Herbs, The Dooryard Herb Cookbook,* and *The Herbal Almanac.* Linda is a columnist and contributing editor to *Virginia Magazine.*

Sources for Illustrations

Following is a partial list of sources for the illustrations contained in this book. These illustrations are woodcuts dating from the eighth through the nineteenth centuries.

Brunschwig. *Liber de arte distillandi*. Strassburg, Gruninger, 1500.

Crescentiis, Petrus. *Das Buch von Pflantzung*. Strasbourg, c. 1497.

Crescientio, Piero. *Agricultura vulgare*. Venice, 1519.

Cuba. *Hortes Sanitatis*. Paris, 1498.

Das Kreterbuch oder Herbarius. Printed by Heinrich Stayner. Augsburg, 1534.

Gerarde, John. *The Herball, or General Historie of Plants*. London: Norton and Whitakers, 1597, 1633.

The grete herball. 1526.

Hortus Saritatis, 1533.

Hugo, Thomas. *Bewick's Woodcuts: Impressions of Upwards of Two Thousand Wood-Blocks, Engraved, For the Most Part, by Thomas and John Bewick of Newcastle-on-Tyne*. London: L. Reeve and Co., 1870.

Hupfuff, Mathias. *Regimen Sanitatis*. Strassburg, 1513.

Johnson, Thomas. *The Herball, etc., of Gerarde*, enlarged and amended. London, 1633.

de L'Obel, Matthias. *Plantarum seu Stirpium adversaria nova*. London, 1570–1571.

Matthiolus, Petrus Andreas. *Commentarii in libros sex Pedacii Dioscoridis*. Venice, 1565.

Monardes. *Segunda parte del libro*. 1571.

Prüss, Johann. *Hortus Saritatus*. Strasbourg, c. 1497.

Schnsperger, Hans. *Kalendar deutsch*. Augsburg, 1484.

Schoeffer, Peter. *Gart der Gesundheit*. Mainz, 1485.
——————. *Hortus Saritatis*. Mainz, 1485.

Strabo, Walafrid. *Hortulus*. Nuremberg, Weyssenburger, 1512.

Vostre, Simon. *Ces presentes heures à l'vsaige de Rome*. Paris, 1498.

Bibliography

Addison, Josephine. *Love Potions: A Book of Charms and Omens.* Topsfield, MA: Salem House Publishers, 1987.

Allordice, Pamela. *Love Potions.* New York: Mallard Press, 1991.

Anderson, Frank J. *An Illustrated History of the Herbals.* New York: Columbia University Press, 1977.

Baker, Margaret. *Discovering the Folklore of Plants.* Tring, Herts, England: Shire Publications, 1969.

Bardswell, Frances A. *The Herb Garden.* Reprint, London: A & C Black Ltd., 1930 (1st ed. 1911).

Baskin, Esther. *The Poppy and Other Deadly Plants.* New York: Delacorte Press, 1967.

Beals, Katharine M. *Flower Lore and Legend.* New York: Henry Holt & Co., 1917.

Beston, Henry. *Herbs and the Earth.* New York: Doubleday Doran and Co., 1935.

Bloom, J. Harvey. *Shakespeare's Garden.* London: Methuen & Co., 1903.

Boland, Bridget. *Gardener's Magic and Other Old Wive's Lore*. New York: Farrar Straux Giroux, 1977.

Boland, Bridget and Maureen Boland. *Old Wives' Lore for Gardeners*. New York: Farrar Straus Giroux, 1977.

Brand, John. *Observations on the Popular Antiquities of Great Britain*. London: Henry G. Bohn, 1853, 1854; reprint, London: Chatto and Windus, 1900.

Budge, Sir E. A. Wallis, *The Divinie Origin of the Craft of the Herbalist*. London: Society of Herbalists, 1928.

Buist, Robert. *The Family Kitchen Garden*. New York: C.M. Saxton & Co., 1855.

Choice Notes from "Notes and Queries": Folklore. London: Bell and Dadly, 1859.

Clarkson, Rosetta I. *Green Enchantment: The Magic Spell of Gardens*. New York: MacMillan, 1940; reprint, *The Golden Age of Herbs and Herbalists*. Dover, New York: Dover Publishing Co., 1972.

_____. *Magic Gardens: A Modern Chronicle of Herbs and Savory Seeds*. New York: MacMillan, 1940; reprint, *Herbs and Savory Seeds*. Dover, New York: Dover Publishing Co., 1940.

Coles, William. *The Art Of Simpling*. Reprint, Milford, CT: Herb Lovers Book Club, 1938 (1st ed. 1656).

Cooper, J.C. *The Aquarian Dictionary of Festivals.* Wellingboro, Northamptonshire: The Aquarian Press, 1990.

Cosman, Madeleine Pelner. *Fabulous Feasts: Medieval Cookery and Ceremony.* New York: George Braziller, Inc., 1976.

Cox, E.H.M. *The Gardener's Chapbook.* London: Chatto and Windus, 1931.

Culpeper, Nicolas. *The British Herbal and Family Physician.* Reprint, London: S. Ballard, R. Ware, et. al., 1741 (1st ed.1649).

Dow, Elaine. *Simples and Worts: Herbs of the American Puritans.* Topsfield, MA: Historical Presentations, 1972.

Dugdale, Rose S. *Fragrant Herbs.* Birmingham, England: Weather Oak Press, 1935.

Durdin-Robertson, Lawrence. *The Year of the Goddess.* Wellingboro, Northamptonshire: The Aquarian Press, 1990.

Ellacombe, Henry N. *Plant Lore and Garden Craft of Shakespeare.* London and New York: Edward Arnold, 1896.

Elworthy, Frederick Thomas. *The Evil Eye.* Secaucus, NJ: University Books-Citadel Press (facsimile 1895 ed.).

Fairbrother, Nan. *Men and Gardens.* New York: Alfred A. Knopf, 1956.

Flint, Martha Bockee. *A Garden of Simples.* New York: Charles Scribner's Sons, 1900.

Frazer, James G. *The New Golden Bough*. Edited by Dr. Theodor H. Gastor. New York: Criterion Books, 1959.

Freeman, Margaret B. *Herbs for the Medieval Household*. New York: Metropolitan Museum of Art, 1943.

Gerard, John. *The Herbal or General Historie of Plantes*. London: John Norton, 1597. Enlarged and amended by Thomas Johnson, 1633. Reprint, New York: Dover Publications, 1975.

Gimbutas, Marija. *The Language of the Goddess*. San Francisco: Harper Collins, 1991.

Gordon, Jean. *Pageant of the Rose*. New York: Studio Associations, 1953.

Gordon, Leslie. *A Country Herbal*. New York: Mayflower Books, 1980.

——————. *Green Magic*. New York: Viking Press, 1977.

Graves, Robert. *The White Goddess*. New York: Octagon Books, 1972.

——————. *The Greek Myths*. Harmondsworth, Middlesex and New York: Penguin Books, 1955; reprinted with amendments, 1957.

Gunther, Robert T. *The Greek Herbal of Dioscordes*. London: Hafner Publishing Co., 1934.

Haddon, Celia. *Be Beautiful the Country Way*. New York: Summit Books, 1978.

Haggard, Ilias Rider. *A Norfolk Notebook*. London: Faber and Faber, 1936.

Halliwell, James Orchard. *Popular Rhymes and Nursery Tales*. London: John Russell Smith, 1849.

Hansen, Harold A. *The Witches Garden*. Translated by Muriel Crofts. York Beach, ME: Samuel Weiser, Inc., 1970.

Harley, Rev. Timothy. *Moon Lore*. Rutland, Vermont and Tokyo, Japan: Charles E. Tuttle & Co., 1970 (1st ed. 1885).

Hartley, Dorothy. *Lost Country Life*. New York: Pantheon Books, 1979.

Hill, Thomas. *The Gardener's Labyrinth*. London: Oxford University Press, 1987 (1st ed. 1577).

Hone, William. *The Table Book of Daily Recreation and Information: Concerning Remarkable Men, Manners, Times, Seasons, Solemnities, Merrymakings, Antiquities, and Novelties Forming a Complete History of the Year and a Perpetual Key to the Almanac*. London: William Tegg, 1827 (2nd ed. 1878).

_____. *Year Book*. London: Ward, Lock, Bowden & Co., 1832 (2nd ed. 1892).

Hylton, William, ed. *The Rodale Herb Book*. Emmaus, PA: Rodale Press, 1974.

Jacob, Dorothy. *A Witches' Guide to Gardening*. New York: Taplinger Publishing Co., 1965.

Jones, Louise S. *Who Loves a Garden*. n.p.: Primavera Press, 1934.

Kamm, Minnie Watson. *Old-Time Herbs for Northern Gardens*. Boston: Little, Brown and Co., 1938.

Keightley, Thomas. *The Fairy Mythology*. Vol. II, London: Whittaker, Treacher and Co., 1833.

Kightly, Charles. *The Perpetual Almanack of Folklore*. New York: Thames and Hudson Ltd., 1987.

Lawson, William. *The Country Housewife's Garden*. Reprint, London: Breslich and Foss, 1983 (1st ed. 1617).

Leighton, Ann. *American Gardens of the Eighteenth Century*. Boston: Houghton Mifflin Co., 1976.

——————. *Early American Gardens*. Boston: Houghton Mifflin Co., 1970.

Leyel, C.F. *Elixirs of Life*. London: Faber and Faber, 1948.

——————. *Herbal Delights*. Reprint, New York: Gramercy Publishing Co., 1986 (1st ed. 1938).

——————. *The Magic of Herbs*. London: Jonathan Cape, 1926.

Logan, Patrick. *Irish Country Cures*. Belfast, Ireland: Appletree Press, 1981.

McLean, Teresa. *Medieval English Gardens*. New York: Viking Press, 1980.

Mondadori, Arnoldo, ed. *The Four Seasons of the House of Cerruti*, from *Sanitatus in Medicina*. 1300, New York: Facts on File Publications, 1984.

Mountainwater, Shekhinah. *Ariadne's Thread*. Freedom, CA: Crossing Press, 1991.

Northcote, Lady Rosalind. *The Book of Herbs*. Dover, New York: Dover Publishing Co., 1971 (1st. ed. 1912).

Parkinson, John. *Paradisi in Sole, Paradisus Terrestris*. Reprint, London: Methuen and Co., 1904 (1st ed. 1621).

Polson, A. *Our Highland Folklore Heritage*. Dingwall, Scotland: George Souter and Inverness, Scotland: Northern Chronicle, 1926.

Rago, Linda O. *Dooryard Herbs*. Shepherdstown, WV: Carabelle Books, 1984.

_____. *Dooryard Herb Cookbook*. Charleston, WV: Pictorial Histories, 1988.

_____. *The Herbal Almanac*. Washington, D.C.: Starwood Publishing, 1992.

Rickert, E. *Ancient English Christmas Carols*. New York: Duffield & Co., 1915.

Rohde, Eleanor Sinclair. *Gardens of Delight*. Boston and New York: Hale, Cushman and Flint, 1936.

_____. *Herbs and Herb Gardening*. New York: MacMillan, 1937.

_____. *The Old-World Pleasaunce*. New York: The Dial Press, 1925.

_____. *Rose Recipes*. London: Routledge, 1939.

_____. *The Scented Garden*. London: Medici Society, 1948.

——————. *Shakespeare's Wild Flower, Fairy Lore, Gatherers of Simples and Bee Lore*. London: Medici Society, N.D.

——————. *The Story of the Garden*. Boston: Hale, Cushman and Flint, 1936.

Simmons, Adelma. *Herb Gardening in Five Seasons*. New York: Hawthorne Press, 1964.

——————. *Herb Gardens of Delight*. New York: Hawthorne Press, 1974.

——————. *A Merry Christmas Herbal*. New York: William Morrow and Co. Inc., 1968.

Simples, Superstitions and Solace, Plant Material Used in Colonial Living. Hartford, CT: National Society of Colonial Dames, 1970.

Singleton, Esther. *The Shakespeare Garden*. New York: William Farquhar Payson, 1931.

Slade, Paddy. *Encyclopedia of White Magic*. New York: Mallard Press, 1990.

Stern, William T. *Botanical Latin*. Newton Abbot: London and North Pomfret, VT: Davis and Charles, 1983.

Strabo, Walafrid. *Hortulus*. Pittsburgh: Hunt Botanical Library, 1966 (facsimile of 840 mss.).

Stuart, David and James Sutherland. *Plants from the Past*. New York: Viking, 1987.

Taberner, Peter V. *Aphrodisiacs: The Science and Myth*. Philadelphia: The University of Pennsylvania Press, 1985.

Thompson, C.J.S. *The Mystic Mandrake*. New Hyde Park, NY: University Books, 1968.

Thorndike, Lynn, Editor. *The Herbal of Rufinus*. Chicago: University of Chicago Press, 1945.

Turner, William. *Herbal*. Arnold Birkman, Collen (Cologne), 1568.

Tusser, Thomas. *Five Hundred Points of Good Husbandry*. Oxford and New York: Oxford University Press, 1984 (1st ed. 1573).

Made in United States
North Haven, CT
02 September 2022

23610351R00082